The Magic of Seeds

Plants

Plants play a **vital** role for all life on Earth. They clean our air. Plants provide shelter, food and medicine.

Plants grow from seeds.

Plants grow in many different environments. Different seeds grow in different conditions and places.

Seeds

Many plants grow from seeds. Seeds are planted in soil. They need sun, water and time to grow into plants.

A tiny seed can grow into a giant tree.

A tree can take years to grow this tall.

Lots of the food we eat starts as a seed. You can grow your own food at home. Home-grown food has lots of flavour.

Saving Seeds

Seed saving is when we keep and store the seeds from plants.

You can save seeds from all sorts of crops, such as vegetables, grains and flowers.

Saved seeds can be used to grow new plants next season.

Some people save seeds to share with their **community**. Swapping seeds with family and friends can help save money.

Although it is more work than getting seeds from a shop, saving seeds is fun.

Seed Saving at Home

Step 1. Collect the seed heads or flowers.

Try saving the seed of your favourite flower.

Step 2. Leave the seeds to dry out completely.

Step 3. Put the dry seeds in a glass jar.

Step 4. Label the seeds.

Step 5. Store the seeds where it is dry, cool and dark. They can last for a year or longer.

It is easy to save your own seeds, though make sure they are stored properly.

Seed Banks

A seed bank is a place where many different sorts of seeds are stored.

A seed bank is a bit like a library for seeds.

Seed banks are important for plant **conservation** and **research**.

Seeds in a seed bank are collected, studied and stored for the future.

The seeds must be stored correctly in cool and dry conditions. This keeps them frozen so they do not rot or sprout.

Seeds can be kept in a seed bank for a long time, even hundreds of years.

Plant **species** face lots of risks. These include disease, natural disasters and changes in climate.

Natural disasters include floods, bushfires and earthquakes.

Scientists at the seed bank help to protect plant species at risk of **extinction**.

The Australian PlantBank

The seeds of rare **native** plant species are stored at The Australian PlantBank.

PlantBank is located in Mount Annan, New South Wales, at the Australian Botanic Garden.

The Australian PlantBank is the biggest native seed bank in Australia. It is also one of the biggest in the world.

A scientist studies seeds closely.

National Indigenous Seed Bank

The National Indigenous Seed Bank also collects and stores native seeds from around Australia.

Australia's First Nations people use native plants in traditional ways.

The National Indigenous Seed Bank aims to educate. This helps to ensure traditional skills are not lost for future generations.

Bush food and plant medicine is an important part of First Nations culture.

Future Food Supply

People rely heavily on crops for the food we eat. Farmers use machines to **plough** their fields and collect the food and seeds. Seeds help to protect the **global** food supply for the future.

Food crops are at risk of both natural disasters and those created by people.

Seed banks could be used to regrow crops if the world needs them.

Global Seed Bank

There is a global seed bank on a remote island. It is located between Norway and the North Pole. Inside are millions of food crop seeds.

There are seeds from almost every country in the world.

The seeds are stored more than 100 metres deep in a mountain. They are surrounded by snow, ice and thick rock. The temperatures are freezing. Even if the power fails, the seeds will stay frozen.

The entire world's food supply is secure.

The Magic of Seeds

Seeds are so important. We can plant seeds at home to grow food and flowers. We can save our favourite seeds for next year.

Seed banks store many seeds for the future. We can study them. We can keep plant species safe from extinction.

Are you a seed-saving champion? Give it a try!

Glossary

community: a group of people living in the same place

conservation: a way of keeping things safe for the future

extinction: when something is at risk of dying out

global: all over the world

native: seeds that grow naturally in an area

plough: dig the ground

research: investigating a special topic

species: a group of living things that are the same

vital: very important

Index